DIGITAL AND INFORMATION LITERACY ™

CYBERBULLYING AND THE LAW

Jefferson Madison
Regional Library
Charlottesville, Virginia

WITHDRAWN

THERESE HARASYMIW

rosen publishing's
rosen
central®

New York

30644 1377

Published in 2013 by The Rosen Publishing Group, Inc.
29 East 21st Street, New York, NY 10010

Copyright © 2013 by The Rosen Publishing Group, Inc.

First Edition

Library of Congress Cataloging-in-Publication Data

Harasymiw, Therese.
Cyberbullying and the law/Therese Harasymiw.
    p. cm.—(Digital and information literacy)
Includes bibliographical references and index.
ISBN 978-1-4488-8359-2 (library binding)—
ISBN 978-1-4488-8366-0 (pbk.)—
ISBN 978-1-4488-8367-7 (6-pack)
1. Cyberbullying—United States. 2. Computer networks—Law and legislation—United States—Criminal provisions. 3. Computer crimes—United States. 4. Teenagers—Legal status, laws, etc.—United States 5. Minors—United States. I. Title.
KF9350.H37 2013
345.73'025—dc23

2012024918

Manufactured in the United States of America

CPSIA Compliance Information: Batch #W13YA: For further information, contact Rosen Publishing, New York, New York, at 1-800-237-9932.

CONTENTS

	Introduction	4
Chapter 1	The Many Kinds of Cyberbullying	7
Chapter 2	Federal Cyber Legislation	12
Chapter 3	State Cyber Legislation	18
Chapter 4	Court Cases and Controversial Decisions	23
Chapter 5	Taking Action	33
	Glossary	38
	For More Information	40
	For Further Reading	42
	Bibliography	44
	Index	46

INTRODUCTION

With the advent of the Internet, new generations of bullies wield words of abuse, not in parks or on playgrounds, but in cyberspace. The menacing "cyberbully" is often anonymous. Incidents of cyberbullying are spreading like a cancer around the world and are having devastating effects on many young victims.

Young people conduct much of their social lives in the realm of cyberspace. A cyberbully can attack his or her victim in a variety of ways. The most common are through e-mails, instant messages, text messages, and images on Web sites. A victim can't walk away without walking away from cyberspace and all of the devices that connect to it.

In 2010, the Cyberbullying Research Center conducted a study of more than 4,400 eleven- to eighteen-year-olds. Researchers asked each participant if he or she had ever been repeatedly mocked or hurt through e-mails, text messages, or online posts. Nearly one in five students surveyed reported being cyberbullied at some point. The Cyberbullying Research Center reports that certain age groups may have victimization rates as high as 40 percent.

People gather to remember Tyler Clementi at Rutgers University in 2010. Clementi killed himself after classmates spied on him via webcam. One of the classmates served time in jail.

News headlines reflect the fact that some young people can't ignore cyberbullies. Many victims are attacked so severely that they believe they cannot overcome the shame. Sometimes the victims do not even know who is bullying them. Tragically, when there seems to be no escape from the pain, some teens choose to take their own lives.

Cyberbullying, by definition, occurs between minors. The government usually leaves the disciplining of young people to families and schools, although the juvenile justice system handles serious situations. However, in the age of cyberbullying, that is changing. Certain cyberbullying activities are already considered criminal under the law, including harassment, pornography, and threats. As more cyberbullying cases are brought to national attention, people are calling for new legislation to police additional bullying behaviors.

Each year, the sense of urgency to halt the growth of cyberbullying increases. People of all ages need to know more about cyberbullying to recognize, prevent, and combat it. Young people need to know what rights they have to protect them in and outside of cyberspace. They need to know how bullying laws are standing up in court. Perhaps most important, they need to know how to be activists rather than victims.

Chapter 1

The Many Kinds of Cyberbullying

Imagine a friend tells you that someone has set up a Facebook profile with your name on it. You sign into Facebook and find an altered photograph mocking you and lies about you written underneath it. People's comments on the profile are cruel and obscene. One commenter said he planned to trip you in school the next day. After reading this, you most likely would feel scared, angry, and embarrassed. You might be unsure what to do to fight back. Unfortunately, similar situations have happened to many young people.

Is It Cyberbullying?

The bullying behavior in the above story is unmistakable, but sometimes cyberbullying is not so clear-cut. One mean comment sent by e-mail is not cyberbullying. An embarrassing photograph transmitted once by cell phone is not necessarily cyberbullying either. Cyberbullying is usually not a single incident; it is often an ongoing activity over a period of time. It is intentional, with the purpose of embarrassing or harming someone. Cyberbullying

Alex Boston, shown here with her parents, was the subject of a fake Facebook profile. Classmates made false, hurtful claims about the fourteen-year-old. The family sued the classmates for libel.

takes place in cyberspace, through communication methods such as e-mail, text message, blogs, and personal Web sites. Online games, especially massively multiplayer online role-playing games (MMORPGs), are another place where bullying occurs. Social networking sites are some of the most common cyberbullying venues.

Direct cyberbullying is easy to recognize. A single threat of bodily harm is cyberbullying. Saying insulting things to someone or about someone online is direct bullying. So is spreading rumors and gossip, whether the information is true or false, especially if it is meant cruelly. Sometimes bullies use several different e-mail accounts to send their messages in order to stay anonymous.

Using someone else's accounts and impersonating him or her is also a form of cyberbullying. A cyberbully may use a person's accounts to make the victim seem like the bully. People then attack the victim online for words or posts that he or she did not even know about. This is called indirect cyberbullying, or cyberbullying by proxy.

Sending threatening or harassing e-mails to someone else is a kind of cyberbullying called cyberstalking. Cyberstalking often takes place between people who have had a previous relationship, on- or offline. It is usually sparked when one person calls off the relationship. However, a cyberstalker may choose his or her victim at random. Cyberstalkers can find personal information, such as addresses and phone numbers, and use this information to their advantage.

"Happy slapping" is yet another type of cyberbullying. It involves someone videotaping another person who is being physically assaulted. The video is then posted online or passed via cell phones for others to see.

Cyberbullies can operate easily because many Web services allow users to remain anonymous. They can use fake names or avatars instead of their real identities. Many people enjoy this anonymity because it gives them a chance to escape the reality of their lives. However, anonymity also allows people to say negative things to others online.

An obvious solution is to prohibit anonymity, and some have tried this route. The popular *World of Warcraft* MMORPG announced in 2010 that its users would have to use their real names to post online. Tens of thousands of gamers complained, however, and the company decided to allow users to keep their anonymity after all. *World of Warcraft*, like many other online games, has policies in place to suspend user privileges if necessary. However, bullying still continues there and in similar online social environments.

Mean, Yes, but Illegal?

In the case of happy slapping, the crime is evident. The victim is physically assaulted. However, other types of cyberbullying involve words. As a legal

File   Edit   View   Favorites   Tools   Help

GRIEFERS, TROLLS, AND THE DISINHIBITED

Griefers, Trolls, and the Disinhibited

"Griefers," "trolls," and the "disinhibited" are terms for people who exhibit certain kinds of behavior online. A griefer is someone who tries to cause online gamers grief, or make their lives unpleasant in the game. Griefers use abusive language and often disrupt the game, even if it affects someone on their team.

A troll is someone who posts comments online in a deliberate attempt to bait someone into a fight. ("Trolling" is a fishing term for dragging bait through the water to catch fish.) Trolls may post off-topic comments or outrageous statements to provoke or inflame others' emotions.

The anonymity of much of the Internet causes many people to feel disinhibited. They act in ways that they never would outside the Web. Griefers and trolls are unpleasant. However, they are just a part of online life that you'd do best to simply ignore—unless they begin to exhibit cyberbullying behaviors.

issue, cyberbullying is often connected to the First Amendment, which states that the government cannot deprive citizens of their right to free speech. However, the U.S. Supreme Court has thoroughly examined the right to free speech since the writing of the Constitution. It has set limitations on this right, including when that speech presents a "clear and present danger."

Some bullying behaviors do present a "clear and present danger" to people's lives—for example, if the bully threatens to hurt or kill his or her victim—and they do not need to be tolerated even once. Slander and libel are also excluded from protection under the First Amendment because they infringe on the rights of others. Some cyberbullying cases involve sexually explicit images. Nude photos of underage minors are considered child

Texting gossip and rumors is a cyberbullying behavior and a major problem among young people today. The origin of the texts may be hard to trace—but not impossible.

pornography, a criminal offense and another activity without constitutional protection.

Since cyberbullying is an issue involving minors, many times schools are the first "court of authority" to address offenses, especially when the bully and victim are both students. Most schools have policies to battle traditional types of schoolyard bullying on their premises. In recent years, they have been creating policies for how to handle cyberbullying, too. However, schools can only deliver the penalties of suspension and expulsion, and they have an obligation to report serious infractions to the police. In 2010, the U.S. Department of Education announced that legal action could be taken against schools that fail to address known bullying and harassment incidents.

Chapter 2

Federal Cyber Legislation

In recent years, people have demanded that federal lawmakers respond to the high incidence of cyberbullying. Some believe that laws criminalizing bullying activities would ensure that harsh action is taken against bullies. Many are pushing for laws at the federal level, since cyberbullying sometimes occurs over state lines, taking it out of an individual state's jurisdiction. Advocates for a federal law believe it would slow the growth of cyberbullying on the Web. To date, the only existing federal laws that directly relate to cyberbullying deal mainly with preventive measures.

Protecting Children in the 21st Century Act

In 2008, the Protecting Children in the 21st Century Act was signed into law. This legislation, also called the Broadband Data Improvement Act, requires that education programs about online sexual predators be implemented in public schools. School districts are also required to develop policies and curricula that promote positive digital citizenship. In other words, they must teach students how to conduct themselves appropriately

In response to federal guidelines, more schools have implemented technology classes focusing on safe Internet use. These Montana students learn how to avoid identity theft and protect themselves against cyberbullying.

while interacting with others online. These measures must also raise awareness of cyberbullying so that students can identify the behavior and learn how they can best respond to it.

While the Protecting Children in the 21st Century Act does not directly define what cyberbullying is and how to combat it, the legislation both authorizes and compels schools to do so.

The Communications Decency Act

The Communications Decency Act of 1996 regulates obscene material on the Internet. Originally, this law was meant to help promote Internet businesses by freeing them from unnecessary lawsuits. Section 203 of the legislation protects Internet service providers (ISPs) and creators of interactive computer services from being held legally responsible for the comments of their users.

However, this measure has become controversial, as it means that companies have little incentive to police their sites and take down hateful messages and other material that violates the rights of others.

Acts About Threatening Messages

The Interstate Communications Act, though originally passed in 1948, has bearing on cyberbullying cases. It made a crime of sending telephone messages and letters that threaten injury over state lines. Now its reach extends to e-mail and instant messages.

The Interstate Stalking and Prevention Act, passed in 1996, makes it illegal for anyone to use the U.S. mail or any computer service across state lines to cause someone major emotional distress.

A part of the Violence Against Women Act, passed in 2000, makes it illegal "to annoy, abuse, harass, or threaten" someone using the telephone or e-mail. Unfortunately, this law does not yet extend to postings on Web sites and Web forums.

Laws such as these often fall short if the victim cannot prove that the stalker or harasser threatened him or her with bodily harm. Cruel words or warnings may not necessarily be considered "true threats" in a court of law, and the definition of "major emotional distress" can vary from court to court.

Falling Short

None of these federal laws make cyberbullying illegal. Only in cases in which the bully or stalker is seen as a real threat will the victim have the possibility of winning a case in court. In recent years, several bills have been presented to Congress in an effort to create a federal cyberbullying law. A stumbling block of cyberbullying laws has been defining exactly what cyberbullying is.

File   Edit   View   Favorites   Tools   Help

     WHO WAS MEGAN MEIER?

Who Was Megan Meier?

The Megan Meier Cyberbullying Prevention Act was a response to the suicide of a young Missouri girl named Megan Meier. Thirteen-year-old Megan met a boy named Josh Evans online through Myspace. Over several weeks, the two exchanged messages, and Meier developed a crush on him. Suddenly, Josh told her that he did not want to be friends. He posted messages calling her fat and told her that the world would be better off without her. Megan, who had previously struggled with self-esteem and depression issues, hanged herself in October 2006.

Several weeks after Megan's death, the Meier family discovered that "Josh Evans" was not real. His Myspace profile had been created by the mother of a former friend of Megan. The mother, Lori Drew, had believed that Megan was spreading rumors about her daughter. She hoped the profile would reveal the truth.

Drew was tried in court under the Computer Fraud and Abuse Act (CFAA) for providing false information to Myspace. The CFAA is a federal law that makes it a crime to access a computer in an unauthorized manner. It is usually applied to businesses and hackers. Drew was cleared of all charges, as a judge ruled that the CFAA did not address this situation.

The Missouri state government and many Missouri local governments created laws to combat cyberbullying after the death of Megan Meier, shown here.

The Megan Meier Cyberbullying Prevention Act, introduced in Congress in 2008, sought to target bullies who send communications via e-mail, instant messaging, blogs, Web sites, telephone, or text messages with the intent to scare, harass, or cause emotional distress to someone. However, the bill was never signed into law. It was thought to have been too broad. The fear was that too many "harmless" Internet users could be prosecuted. Additionally, it did not answer key questions. How many times does a bully need to send a message before he or she is punished? What words or ideas make a message a crime?

Targeting Higher Education

The Tyler Clementi Higher Education Anti-Harassment Act of 2011 is named for an eighteen-year-old Rutgers University student. Tyler Clementi, who was

Tyler Clementi's mother looks at photos of her son after his suicide. Clementi is now a symbol for antibullying legislation, in particular laws targeting hate crimes involving sexual orientation.

gay, committed suicide after his roommate and another student used a Webcam to secretly stream video of him in his room with a male date.

The proposed measure named for Clementi would require any college receiving federal money to prohibit harassment of students based on race, color, nationality, sex, disability, sexual orientation, or religion. Colleges would need to establish preventive programs educating students on cyberbullying, as well as provide services to victims. The bill failed to pass initially. However, many in Congress vow to keep fighting for its adoption.

MYTH The First Amendment of the U.S. Constitution means that cyberbullies can say whatever they want.

FACT The First Amendment, which includes the right to free speech, protects reasonable speech. Threats and certain other kinds of expression do not fall under this umbrella.

MYTH All schools must respect a student's right to free speech.

FACT Private schools do not function as part of the government in the same way that public schools do. They may place more limitations on students' freedom of expression.

MYTH If a cyberbully is under eighteen, he or she cannot go to jail for his or her actions.

FACT Minors are often tried in juvenile courts and may face jail time depending on the seriousness of the crime.

Chapter 3

State Cyber Legislation

Even though no federal anticyberbullying law is currently in place, the majority of state legislatures have addressed online bullying in recent years. Most states don't go as far as labeling cyberbullying a crime. However, a few have—Rhode Island, Idaho, and North Carolina identify the first offense as a misdemeanor. As of May 2012, forty-nine of fifty states had some type of antibullying legislation. The only state without a law was Montana.

Much of the state legislation speaks to the responsibilities of elementary and high schools in preventing and combating cyberbullying. While this puts the burden of defining cyberbullying on school districts (and opens them to parental lawsuits), it also gives schools the power to mold policies to the specific needs of the student body. In the United States, all young people are entitled to a public education. Under that directive, schools are expected to provide a safe learning environment, including a safe online environment for students.

Groundbreaking State Laws

In 2008, California gave power to superintendents and principals through Education Code 48900 to suspend or expel a student from school for

Responsible use of the Internet is becoming an essential—and even mandatory—part of the technology curriculum.

cyberbullying other students or school personnel while on school grounds; while traveling to or coming from school; during the lunch period, whether on or off campus; or during, on the way to, or on the way from a school-sponsored activity. The specified times are in response to cases in which schools tried to expel students but could not because the bullying occurred off school grounds.

Delaware's School Bullying Prevention Act of 2007 allows a school to take action against a cyberbully, even if the harassment occurs away from school grounds, as long as the bullying is disturbing the school environment. Georgia, Massachusetts, and Illinois have similar legislation.

File   Edit   View   Favorites   Tools   Help

AVOIDING ACCIDENTAL CYBERBULLYING

Avoiding Accidental Cyberbullying

Sometimes people get drawn into cyberbullying. Users should be careful about how they disagree with others on the Web. Computer users of all ages get caught up in heated online discussions about the greatest quarter-back of all time or the latest presidential election. It is best to stick to the facts and never attack someone personally.

People often get emotional when responding to someone who is unreasonable or acting like a troll or griefer. If a discussion gets passionate, sometimes it is better to log off and walk away rather than respond. A single argument can escalate into cyberbullying, especially in places where people may "meet" again and again. Remember, your comments may be saved online indefinitely. Additionally, misunderstandings can result from comments meant as jokes. People should always ask themselves how another person might read a comment.

Other ways to avoid "accidental" cyberbullying include not forwarding e-mails without first asking the person who wrote the e-mail. The person's words could be taken out of context. Similarly, do not post pictures of friends without asking them first. Finally, never reply to a message from a cyberbully. A reply of anger may be used against you. Just collect the electronic evidence in case you need proof of the bullying in the future.

In Florida, the Jeffrey Johnston Stand Up for All Students Act of 2008 was named for fifteen-year-old Jeffrey Johnston, who took his own life after being bullied online over a span of two years. This legislation is similar to Delaware's law but expands the scope of the harassment to include its effects on the victim's performance at school.

In New York, the Dignity for All Students Act of 2010 bans harassment and discrimination against students based on sexual orientation, gender, race, color, weight, national origin, ethnicity, religion, or mental or physical disability. It requires each school district in the state to adopt antibullying measures and implement preventive education programs. Administrators must report incidents of bullying to the state education department.

New Jersey's Anti-Bullying Bill of Rights, which went into effect at the start of the 2011 school year, is the first law to require public universities to distribute antibullying policies to students. It also requires training courses for school personnel and disciplinary action for failure to report incidents. (This legislation garnered public support after the suicide of New Jersey college student Tyler Clementi.)

In 2012, South Dakota became the forty-ninth state to enact cyberbullying legislation. The law provides schools with a bullying policy until they craft their own.

Rhode Island's cyberbullying legislation, passed in 2008, is some of the toughest to date. The measure labels a first offense for electronic harassment a misdemeanor. Convicted cyberbullies face a possible $500 fine and up to a year in prison. A second offense is a felony, punishable by up to two years in prison and $6,000 in fines.

Other states are currently debating legislation similar to Rhode Island's, hoping to send a stronger message about the seriousness of cyberbullying. In New York, state senators are considering a bill defining "bullycide," which would target people who bully with the intent to cause their victims to commit suicide. If the legislation passes, cyberbullies would be charged with second-degree manslaughter.

Cyberbullying Activists

Lawmakers often take on the causes brought to their attention by their constituents. Many cyberbullying activists are among those who have

John Halligan speaks to a student assembly about his son, who killed himself after being bullied online. Halligan encourages young people to take action to stop the growing problem.

been most deeply affected by the problem. Parents such as Tina Meier, Megan's mother, and John Halligan, whose son Ryan committed suicide after being bullied online, pushed for new laws in their states because of the tragedies they experienced. Clementi's family lent their son's name to the federal bill awaiting a decision—the Tyler Clementi Higher Education Anti-Harassment Act.

With each legislative session, states are continuously updating their bullying and cyberbullying laws in response to the needs of their citizens. Residents can find new laws by checking their state department of education's Web site or their state legislature's Web site.

→ **Chapter 4**

Court Cases and Controversial Decisions

ourts are testing state and federal legislation concerning cyberbullying and related issues, such as student free speech. Real-life cases bring to light the strengths and weaknesses in the legislative measures, as well as in the policies of school districts. Most cyberbullying incidents are handled at school, and many of the following cases involve conflicts between students and schools. If a student or a student's parents disagree with a school's decision, they may take the school to court.

Free Speech in School

Public school students do have free speech rights. *Tinker v. Des Moines Independent Community School District* (1969) is the most famous case regarding students' rights to free expression. The U.S. Supreme Court declared that three Iowa teens had the right to wear black armbands in school as a way to protest the Vietnam War. The Court's decision included this thought: "It can hardly be argued that either students or teachers shed

Avery Doninger *(center)* took her school to court after it barred her from running for class office. She maintained the school had no right to discipline her for comments in her off-campus blog. The court disagreed.

their constitutional rights to freedom of speech or expression at the schoolhouse gate."

However, as has already been noted, not all speech and expression are protected under law. In the *Tinker* decision, the Court said that school officials can prohibit speech that would cause a "substantial disruption" in the school environment or "invade the rights of others." But, the Court said, the students' act of wearing armbands to express their political views did not meet that description.

Off-Campus Speech

In many court cases involving student speech today, the question is whether schools can exert control over student expression when students are off school grounds. Can schools regulate student cyber speech at home? What if that speech would create a substantial disruption at school? Several cases have argued this point.

Sixteen-year-old Avery Doninger was at home writing her personal blog when she criticized her school for postponing an event. However, she used language deemed offensive by school officials who, as an act of punishment, refused to let her run for class office the following year. Avery maintained that her right to free speech allowed her to write whatever she wanted in her blog at home. In *Avery Doninger v. Lewis Mills High School* (2008), a federal court ruled that the school did not abuse its power in keeping Avery from running for office. According to the court, Avery had no right to hold office. In addition, her language affected the school environment. An appeal to the U.S. Supreme Court was denied.

In another case, eighth-grader Jill Snyder was at home when she created a fake Myspace profile for her principal. She made up outrageous details about his life, including his sexual activities. When the principal found out, Jill was suspended for ten days. The student took the school to court twice and lost both times. One federal court claimed that Jill's right to free speech did not extend to the graphic sexual content of her made-up profile. However, in a third case, an appeal to the U.S. Court of Appeals, Jill was the victor. In *Blue Mountain School District v. Snyder* (2011), the federal court ruled that she was protected under the First Amendment and that the fake profile was not a significant disruption to school life.

Clearly, the results of these cases are in conflict. As the U.S. Supreme Court did not hear either of the appeals, lower courts will continue to rule as they see fit.

"Real Threats"

If a school system finds that the behavior of a cyberbully calls for a punishment more severe than expulsion, school officials may involve the criminal

Anthony Latour *(left)* was removed from his school after he posted violent song lyrics online that school officials believed were threats. However, the courts ruled that no clear threat existed.

justice system. Young people charged with crimes are usually tried as juveniles if they are under a certain age (such as sixteen or eighteen). However, depending on the state and the offense, a juvenile may be tried as an adult in a criminal court, which means stiffer sentences if proven guilty. Certain kinds of cyberbullying involve conduct understood to be real threats of violence and such threats are criminal. But what is considered "real"?

Dylan Mardis told friends through an instant message (IM) chat that he was planning to bring a gun to school and shoot certain people, whom he named. When the communications were reported, he was suspended from school. Because of the serious nature of the threats, he spent time in juvenile detention. Dylan lost an appeal in federal court. In *D. J. M. v. Hannibal Public School District #80* (2011), the court ruled that "real threats" are not covered under the right to free speech and that the school could not be expected to wait to see if Dylan intended to carry out his plans.

The case *Joshua Mahaffey v. Waterford School District* (2002) involved a fifteen-year-old who created a Web page on which he listed several students under the heading, "People I Wish Would Die." Though criminal charges were not filed, Joshua Mahaffey spent some time being evaluated at a psychiatric hospital. He was cleared to go back to school but was then suspended. Joshua and his parents sued, citing freedom of expression. The court ruled in the student's favor, as it did not see his Web site as a "true threat." He did not say he was actually going to kill or harm anyone.

In *Anthony Latour v. Riverside Beaver School District* (2005) and the *Matter of Singh* (2003), students were taken out of school because they had written songs outside of school that included violent lyrics about school officials. However, neither student was found to be a true threat to officials. In these cases, their right to express themselves was upheld.

Pornographic Material, Sexting, and Other Crimes

Sexting—sending or receiving sexually explicit images or texts—is becoming a more common activity among young people today. However, when photo subjects are minors, the material may be labeled child pornography, which is a crime to possess and distribute.

Cyberbullying cases involving sexting often stem from broken relationships. In *State v. Alpert* (2008), eighteen-year-old Philip Alpert was convicted of distributing child pornography for sending nude photos of his minor ex-girlfriend to more than seventy people after a bad breakup. Alpert will be a registered sex offender until he is forty-three.

| File | Edit | View | Favorites | Tools | Help |

ARE WEB SITES RESPONSIBLE FOR BULLYING?

Are Web Sites Responsible for Bullying?

In some circumstances of cyberbullying, it may seem appropriate to hold the Web site that allows the bullying to take place partly responsible. Ryan Dwyer, an eighth grader in New Jersey, created a Web site on which he criticized his school, calling it the "worst school on the planet." While he encouraged others to add comments, he warned them not to use profanity or write threats. His warnings were ignored, however, and Ryan's principal found threats and obscene language against both the school and himself on the site. After Ryan was disciplined and suspended, he and his parents took the school to court. In *Ryan Dwyer v. Oceanport District* (2005), the court found in Ryan's favor because he did not write the threats or profanity himself.

The decision also upheld the Communications Decency Act, stating that creators of interactive Web services are not responsible for content added by outsiders. Similarly, Facebook and Myspace are not legally responsible for bullying content on their forums. According to a number of court decisions, they are not even liable for failing to remove content after it has been discovered. However, these sites may delete posts as a courtesy to their users. Facebook has even developed a procedure to help young people report cyberbullying more easily.

Girls as young as thirteen have been charged with distributing child pornography for sending nude photos of themselves to boys. In at least one case, the recipients, just two years older, were charged with possession of child pornography. In some cases, such as *Miller v. Skumanik* (2009), prosecutors offer young defendants such as these reduced charges in exchange for completing counseling, sex education programs, and community service. (In the *Miller* case, the photos had been circulating for two years before a school official found them on a student's cell phone.)

The law takes child pornography issues very seriously, even if young people themselves are the source. There are some calls for legislation to control sexting, though others believe it is an issue best left to schools and parents.

Bullying to the Point of Suicide

The case of Phoebe Prince is one of the first in which minors faced criminal charges for harassment of a classmate. Five Massachusetts teenagers faced multiple indictments, including harassing and stalking the fifteen-year-old. Phoebe was bullied on Twitter, Craigslist, Facebook, and Formspring, and she was tormented through text messages as well. She was also physically bullied. Phoebe hanged herself after school in 2010. To avoid harsher sentences, all of the accused pleaded guilty to the charges and were sentenced to probation and community service. Many people, hearing the specifics of the case, thought they were excused too easily.

The 2010 suicide of fourteen-year-old Jamey Rodemeyer uncovered his history of being cyberbullied. According to *ABC News*, anonymous posts on Formspring included: "JAMIE IS STUPID, GAY, FAT ANND [sic] UGLY. HE MUST DIE!" Another read, "I wouldn't care if you died. No one would. So just do it :) It would make everyone WAY more happier!"

However, a criminal case was not filed against his attackers. The district attorney's office said it lacked evidence showing a repeated pattern

Classmates of Massachusetts teenager Phoebe Prince sit in court. They were charged with and pleaded guilty to harassing Phoebe, who committed suicide in 2010.

of abuse by any one person. In the *Buffalo News*, the district attorney stated, "The evidence, at best, was very thin. It's not a crime to be an obnoxious, teenage idiot." Unfortunately, the best witness to the bullying was no longer able to speak up—Jamey Rodemeyer himself.

The Verdict

These cases above demonstrate that one can take legal action against cyberbullies who use threats against schools and people's lives. The law also resolutely acts against child pornography. However, when a cyberbully's messages are viewed as "merely" crude, mean, or unpleasant, the victim is often left more vulnerable.

Schools, though, are beginning to support victims of all kinds of cyberbullying. Many schools have an acceptable use policy for their computers and computer systems to which parents and students must agree. By adding a condition that covers abusive actions by students, the school can give itself greater authority—under a binding contract—to take appropriate action to deal with cyberbullying. Still, the scope of a school's authority varies depending on its state laws and whether the action takes place on or off its grounds. This should not deter cyberbullying victims from empowering themselves and taking action.

TEN GREAT QUESTIONS
TO ASK A SCHOOL GUIDANCE COUNSELOR

1. What is the difference between teasing and bullying?

2. When should I ignore a cyberbully?

3. How can I help a friend get help if he or she is being cyberbullied?

4. How can I stop a friend from cyberbullying others?

5. How can the school help someone who is being cyberbullied?

6. What if I am being cyberbullied when I am not at school?

7. At what point will the school call the police about a case of cyberbullying?

8. What should I do if someone else is using my e-mail or online profile to bully?

9. What should I do if people have photos of me that I do not want them to have?

10. How can our school get involved in fighting cyberbullying?

Chapter 5

Taking Action

If a young person believes he or she is a victim of cyberbullying, there are several steps to take to mount a successful effort for justice. The Web site StopCyberbullying.com suggests remembering the phrase "Stop, block, and tell." That means a user should "stop" himself or herself from responding to bullies, "block" the e-mail address or IM account, and then "tell" an adult. A user should not respond to a threatening message. Often cyberbullies want a response, and a reply written in a moment of anger may be turned against the user. The bully can claim that the victim initiated the fight and use the angry reactions as evidence.

Document the Bullying

While refraining from replying, the victim (or the victim's parents) should keep the cyberbullying messages. They can be used as evidence if the victim needs to make a case against the bully later on. As in any U.S. court, the accused is innocent until proven guilty. As painful as it may be to save cruel and demeaning e-mails or texts, these items are the proof needed to mount a successful case. Relevant Web pages should be downloaded and online chats copied or saved.

File a Complaint

Cyberbullying may violate the "terms of use" or "acceptable use policy" of a Web site, Internet service provider (ISP), or cell phone company. This is an agreement stating what users may—and may not—do with the Web service. Many social networking and gaming sites and chat rooms have policies about bullying. Users are often able to submit a formal complaint against another account, especially if they have proof of wrongdoing, such as a link to offending messages. Victims can request that an account be discontinued. Not only does this help the victim, it also helps other victims of the bully who did not come forward. Removing bullies also helps maintain a positive

School counselors are trained to help students cope with bullying and cyberbullying. They can also help start the process of action against the bully.

atmosphere on Web sites. Users should request the deletion of offensive material from sites, too.

Involve the School

If the victim knows or suspects that a student is the bully, the school should be informed. The school's response will depend on the local law, the school's cyberbullying policy, and when and where the bullying took place. A school may not be able to discipline a student for off-campus actions. However, if the cyberbully is using the school's Internet account or computers or is bullying at school, the victim can expect support. In many states, the school can intervene with formal discipline, even if these conditions are not met, especially if the school environment has been disrupted or the victim's academic performance has been affected negatively. Victims should examine the school's acceptable-use Internet policy as well as state laws.

The school can also contact the parents of the cyberbully. The cyberbully's parents or guardians may be unaware of the bully's activities and may be willing to intercede.

Unmask the Bully

Many people who are bullied online did not do anything to invite the abuse. They may not know why they are being bullied. They may not even know for sure who is bullying them. Some cyberbullies pretend to be someone else, so it is vital to get the truth.

Text messages can be traced back to a cyberbully through telephone companies. A cyberbully's online comments can be traced through his or her computer's Internet protocol (IP) address. A school may have a district technology director who can search district Internet records if the bully is using school property. An ISP can also find the source. However, if the cyberbullying is likely to be considered a crime, the police may take responsibility for tracking the IP address.

File   Edit   View   Favorites   Tools   Help

IS INTERNET PRIVACY POSSIBLE?

Is Internet Privacy Possible?

The first line of defense against cyberbullying for users of social networking sites is the site's privacy settings. Certain settings make it difficult for unauthorized people to contact users or view their information. For example, settings on Facebook can keep messages, photos, and other bits of information from being seen by anyone other than people the user approves. However, users often need to change these settings, as the default setting may let anyone see their profiles.

With any online profile, the user should not post information that is too personal. Friends and family already know where the user lives, as well as his or her phone number, so this information is unnecessary. Photos may also be targets for online bullies as well as sexual predators. Internet users should consider whether privacy is ever really possible on the Internet, when hackers are able to compromise well-protected databases of major companies and even the federal government.

When Do You Need an Attorney?

An attorney can be a victim's representative, asking a cyberbully's parents to stop their child's actions. He or she can recommend resources to identify the bully's IP address. An attorney can help victims get an injunction to stop the behavior and remove the harmful messages or images. He or she can also provide information about whether the cyberbullying would be grounds for a potential lawsuit for financial compensation.

The Internet can be part of the cyberbullying solution, too. Many sites, such as StopBullying .gov (http://www.stopbullying.gov), are available to inform young people about the issue and provide support.

Contact the Police

If the cyberbullying appears to be a crime, contact the police. Criminal cyberbullying includes, but is not limited to, threats of violence, coercion, obscenity, harassment, stalking, hate and bias crimes, the creation and sending of sexually explicit pictures, and child pornography.

By taking action, victims of cyberbullying will not only help themselves overcome their feelings of powerlessness, they will also be standing up for future potential victims.

GLOSSARY

anonymous Not named or identified.

avatar A movable, three-dimensional image used to represent an individual in cyberspace, especially in multiplayer games, online communities, and Web forums.

coercion The use of force or threats to make someone do something.

constituent Any of the people who live and vote in an area.

default An option that will automatically be selected by a computer if the user does not choose one.

disinhibit To lose or remove self-restraint.

explicit Portraying nudity, sexual activity, or violence in an open and direct way.

felony A serious crime, such as murder, that is punished more severely than a misdemeanor.

hacker A person who uses computer skills to gain unauthorized access to a computer system.

harassment The act of persistently annoying, attacking, or bothering someone.

impersonate To pretend to be another person.

indictment A formal accusation of a serious crime.

injunction A court order that requires a person to do something or stop doing something.

IP address The numeric address of a computer on the Internet.

libel A false and malicious published statement that damages someone's reputation.

manslaughter The unlawful killing of a person by another without advance planning.

minor A person who is not yet old enough to have the legal rights and responsibilities of an adult.

misdemeanor A crime less serious than a felony and resulting in a less severe punishment.

obscene Offensive to standards of decency, especially by being sexually explicit.

pornography Films, magazines, writings, photographs, or other materials that are sexually explicit.

prosecute To bring civil or criminal court action against.

slander The act of saying something false or malicious that damages someone's reputation.

try To carry out a trial to decide if someone is innocent or guilty of a crime or offense.

FOR MORE INFORMATION

Cyberbullying Research Center
School of Criminology and Criminal Justice
Florida Atlantic University
5353 Parkside Drive
Jupiter, FL 33458-2906
Web site: http://www.cyberbullying.us/index.php
The Cyberbullying Research Center was founded to provide up-to-date infor-
     mation about the issue of cyberbullying among young people. It offers
     helpful resources for teens, parents, and educators.

First Amendment Center
555 Pennsylvania Avenue
Washington, DC 20001
(202) 292-6288
Web site: http://www.firstamendmentcenter.org
The First Amendment Center is an online forum for the study of free-expression
     issues, including freedom of speech.

Massachusetts Aggression Reduction Center
Bridgewater State University
131 Summer Street
Bridgewater, MA 02324
(508) 531-1784
Web site: http://webhost.bridgew.edu/marc
The Massachusetts Aggression Reduction Center is an academic center that
     provides services and programs about bullying and cyberbullying
     prevention to schools.

PREVNet
Queen's University
98 Barrie Street
Kingston, ON K7L 3N6
Canada
(866) 372-2495
Web site: http://prevnet.ca
PREVnet is a national network of Canadian researchers and organizations
sharing resources to stop bullying.

WiredKids, Inc.
PMB 342
4401-A Connecticut Avenue NW
Washington, DC 20008
(201) 463-8663
Web site: http://www.stopcyberbullying.org
This organization provides information for children and parents on how to
recognize cyberbullying, how to prevent it, and what the law is regarding cyberbullying.

Web Sites

Due to the changing nature of Internet links, Rosen Publishing has developed
an online list of Web sites related to the subject of this book. This site is
updated regularly. Please use this link to access the list:

http://www.rosenlinks.com/DIL/Bully

FOR FURTHER READING

Allman, Toney. *Mean Behind the Screen: What You Need to Know About Cyberbullying* (What's the Issue?). Minneapolis, MN: Compass Point Books, 2009

Billitteri, Thomas J. *Cyberbullying: Are New Laws Needed to Curb Online Aggression?* (CQ Researcher). Washington, DC: Congressional Quarterly, 2008.

Bissonette, Aimée M. *Cyber Law: Maximizing Safety and Minimizing Risk in Classrooms.* Thousand Oaks, CA: Corwin Press, 2009.

Breguet, Teri. *Frequently Asked Questions About Cyberbullying* (FAQ: Teen Life). New York, NY: Rosen Publishing, 2007.

Espejo, Roman. *Social Networking* (Teen Rights and Freedoms). Farmington Hills, MI: Greenhaven Press, 2012.

Friedman, Lauri S. *Cyberbullying* (Introducing Issues with Opposing Viewpoints). Farmington Hills, MI: Greenhaven Press, 2011.

Gerdes, Louise I. *Cyberbullying* (At Issue). Farmington Hills, MI: Greenhaven Press, 2012.

Hinduja, Sameer, and Justin W. Patchin. *Bullying Beyond the Schoolyard: Preventing and Responding to Cyberbullying.* Thousand Oaks, CA: Corwin Press, 2009.

Hunter, Nick. *Cyber Bullying* (Hot Topics). Chicago, IL: Heinemann Library, 2012.

Jacobs, Thomas A. *Teen Cyberbullying Investigated: Where Do Your Rights End and Consequences Begin?* Minneapolis, MN: Free Spirit Publishing, 2010.

Kiesbye, Stefan. *Sexting* (At Issue). Farmington Hills, MI: Greenhaven Press, 2011.

MacEachern, Robyn, and Geraldine Charette. *Cyberbullying: Deal with It and Ctrl Alt Delete It* (Deal with It). Toronto, Canada: J. Lorimer & Co., 2008.

McQuade, Samuel C., Sarah Gentry, Nathan W. Fisk, and Marcus K. Rogers. *Cyberstalking and Cyberbullying* (Cybersafety). New York, NY: Chelsea House, 2012.

Roleff, Tamara L., ed. *Cyberbullying* (Issues That Concern You). Farmington Hills, MI: Greenhaven Press, 2012.

Shariff, Shaeen. *Confronting Cyber-Bullying: What Schools Need to Know to Control Misconduct and Avoid Legal Consequences.* New York, NY: Cambridge University Press, 2009.

Shariff, Shaheen. *Cyber-Bullying: Issues and Solutions for the School, the Classroom and the Home.* New York, NY: Routledge, 2008.

Strauss, Susan. *Sexual Harassment and Bullying: A Guide to Keeping Kids Safe and Holding Schools Accountable.* Lanham, MD: Rowman & Littlefield Publishers, 2012.

Willard, Nancy E. *Cyberbullying and Cyberthreats: Responding to the Challenge of Online Social Aggression, Threats, and Distress.* Champaign, IL: Research Press, 2007.

BIBLIOGRAPHY

Anti-Defamation League (ADL). "ADL Cyberbullying Resource Center—Understanding and Addressing Online Bullying." 2012. Retrieved February 6, 2012 (http://www.adl.org/cyberbullying).

Carvin, Andy. "CA Legislation Criminalizes Campus Cyberbullying." PBS Teachers, August 29, 2008. Retrieved January 13, 2012 (http://www.pbs.org/teachers/learning.now/2008/08/ca_legislation_criminalizes_ca.html).

CircuitSplits.com. "Case Page: *Blue Mountain School District v. Snyder.*" November 24, 2011. Retrieved December 31, 2011 (http://www.circuitsplits.com/us-court-of-appeals-for-the-third-circuit).

Debucquoy-Dodley, Dominique. "New York Looks to 'Modernize' Cyberbullying Laws." CNN, September 27, 2011. Retrieved February 2, 2012 (http://articles.cnn.com).

Donlin, Mike. "The Protecting Children in the 21st Century Act—a Re-Introduction." InsidetheSchool.com, November 9, 2011. Retrieved February 6, 2012 (http://www.insidetheschool.com).

Hinduja, Sameer, and Justin W. Patchin. "Cyberbullying Fact Sheet: Identification, Prevention, and Response." Cyberbullying Research Center, 2010. Retrieved January 7, 2012 (http://www.cyberbullying.us/Cyberbullying_Identification_Prevention_Response_Fact_Sheet.pdf).

Hinduja, Sameer, and Justin W. Patchin. "Responding to Cyberbullying: Top Ten Tips for Teens." Cyberbullying Research Center, January 2012. Retrieved February 27, 2012 (http://www.cyberbullying.us/Top_Ten_Tips_Teens_Response.pdf).

Jacobs, Natalie. "10 Student Free Speech Cases." AsktheJudge.info, August 30, 2011. Retrieved February 2, 2012 (http://www.askthejudge.info).

Jacobs, Thomas A. "Off-Campus Bullying Addressed by Only 13 States." AsktheJudge.info, January 1, 2012. Retrieved February 6, 2012 (http://www.askthejudge.info/off-campus-bullying-addressed-by-only-13-states/12175).

Lavers, Michael K. "New York Anti-Bullying Bill Becomes Law." EDGE
    Boston, September 8, 2010. Retrieved January 13, 2012 (http://
    www.edgeboston.com/index.php?ch=news&sc=&sc3=&id=110059).
Megan Meier Cyberbullying Prevention Act, H.R. 1966, 111th Cong. 1st
    Sess. (2009).
Nowak, Peter. "World of Warcraft Gamers Can Stay Anonymous." *CBC News*,
    July 12, 2010. Retrieved January 13, 2012 (http://www.cbc.ca/news
    /technology/story/2010/07/12/blizzard-world-of-warcraft-forums.html).
Rose, Veronica. "OLR Research Report: Cyberstalking." State of Connecticut
    General Assembly, February 23, 2009. Retrieved December 31,
    2011 (http://www.cga.ct.gov/2009/rpt/2009-R-0117.htm).
Salem Police Department (Massachusetts). "CyberBullying Prevention."
    Retrieved January 13, 2012 (http://salempd.net/Cyberbullying.htm).
Schworm, Peter. "'Blind Eye to Bullying' Over, DA Says." *Boston Globe*, May
    6, 2011. Retrieved February 6, 2012 (http://www.boston.com).
Tan, Sandra. "Police Close Rodemeyer Case with No Arrests." *Buffalo
    News*, November 23, 2011. Retrieved December 31, 2011 (http://
    www.buffalonews.com/topics/school-bullying/article644397.ece).
University of North Carolina School of Law. "Cyberbullying and Criminal
    Laws." 2010. Retrieved December 31, 2011 (http://www.unc.edu/
    courses/2010spring/law/357c/001/Cyberbully/criminal.html).
WiredKids, Inc. "Cyberbullying by Proxy." StopCyberbullying.org. Retrieved
    January 3, 2012 (http://www.stopcyberbullying.org/how_it_works/
    cyberbullying_by_proxy.html).
WiredKids, Inc. "Direct Attacks." StopCyberbullying.org. Retrieved January
    3, 2012 (http://www.stopcyberbullying.org/how_it_works/direct
    _attacks.html).
WiredKids, Inc. "What Is Cyberbullying, Exactly?" StopCyberbullying.org.
    Retrieved January 3, 2012 (http://www.stopcyberbullying.org/what_
    is_cyberbullying_exactly.html).

INDEX

A

Alpert, Philip, 28
Anti-Bullying Bill of Rights (New Jersey), 21

B

Blue Mountain School District v. Snyder, 25

C

child pornography, 10–11, 28–29, 31
Clementi, Tyler, 16–17, 21, 22
Communications Decency Act, 13–14, 28
Computer Fraud and Abuse Act, 15
cyberbullying
    "accidental," 20
    identifying, 7–9
    indirect, 9
    school policies, 11, 12–13, 18, 23,
        31, 35
    Web sites and, 8, 9, 14, 28,
        34–35, 36
cyberstalking, 9

D

Dignity for All Students Act (New York), 21
disinhibited, the, 10
*D. J. M. v. Hannibal Public School
    District #80*, 27
Doninger, Avery, 25
Doninger v. Lewis Mills High School, 25
Dwyer, Ryan, 28
Dwyer v. Oceanport District, 28

E

Education Code 48900 (California),
    18–19

F

First Amendment/freedom of speech,
    10, 17, 23–25

G

griefers, 10

H

Halligan, John, 22
happy slapping, 9

I

indirect cyberbulling/cyberbullying
        by proxy, 9
Interstate Communications Act, 14
Interstate Stalking and Prevention Act, 14

J

Jeffrey Johnston Stand Up for All Students
        Act (Florida), 20
Johnston, Jeffrey, 20

L

*Latour v. Riverside Beaver School
        District*, 27
libel, 10

M

Mahaffey, Joshua, 27
*Mahaffey v. Waterford School
    District*, 27
Mardis, Dylan, 27
Megan Meier Cyberbullying Prevention
    Act, 15, 16
Meier, Megan, 15, 22
Meier, Tina, 22
Miller v. Skumanik, 29

O

off-campus speech, 25

P

Prince, Phoebe, 29
Protecting Children in the 21st
    Century Act, 12–13

R

"real threats" of violence, 26–27
Rodemeyer, Jamey, 29–30

S

School Bullying Prevention Act
    (Delaware), 19
sexting, 27–29
Singh, Matter of, 27
slander, 10
Snyder, Jill, 25
State v. Alpert, 28
suicide, 5, 21, 29–30

T

*Tinker v. Des Moines Independent
    Community School District*,
    23–25
trolls, 10
Tyler Clementi Higher Education Anti-
    Harassment Act, 16, 22

V

Violence Against Women Act, 14

W

World of Warcraft, 9

About the Author

Therese Harasymiw, a former educator, is an author and editor of more than one hundred children's nonfiction books, including several on the Bill of Rights and the U.S. Constitution. A graduate of Providence College, Harasymiw holds an M.A. in English education from the State University of New York at Buffalo. She currently resides in Atlanta, Georgia, with her husband, Mark.

Photo Credits